# A New True Book

# OTTERS

**By Emilie U. Lepthien**

CHILDRENS PRESS®
CHICAGO

River otters looking
out of their den

PHOTO CREDITS

© Erwin and Peggy Bauer–2

© Reinhard Brucker–Field Museum, Chicago,
40 (2 photos)

© Alan & Sandy Carey–19 (left), 32

GeoIMAGERY–© Erwin C. Bud Nielsen–10

H. Armstrong Roberts–© T. Ulrich–7 (bottom
right)

© Jerry Hennen–19 (right),

© Tom & Pat Leeson–33

North Wind Picture Archives–37, 39

Photri–© Lee Rue Jr., 14

Tom Stack & Associates–© Thomas Kitchin,
6 (right); © John Shaw, 22; © Jeff Foott, 29

© Lynn M. Stone–43

Tony Stone Images–© Manfred Danegger,
7 (left)

SuperStock International, Inc.–© Leonard
Lee Rue III, 4; © Charlie Heidecker, 9

Valan–© Fred Bruemmer, 5; © Wayne
Lankinen, 6 (left), 8; © J.A. Wilkinson, 7
(top right); © Michael J. Johnson, 13; © Wilf
Schurig, 15; © Stephen J. Krasemann, 16,
31 (left), 34 (left); © Kennon Cooke, 18; © Jeff
Foott, 25, 31 (right), 34 (right), 36, 45;
© John Cancalosi, 28, 44 (top)

Visuals Unlimited–© Stephen J. Lang, Cover;
© D. & M. Long, 20; © John Gerlach,
27; © Milton H. Tierney, Jr., 44 (bottom)

COVER: River otters

Project Editor: Fran Dyra
Design: Margrit Fiddle

Library of Congress Cataloging-in-Publication Data

Lepthien, Emilie U. (Emilie Utteg)
    Otters / by Emilie U. Lepthien.
        p.      cm.–(A New true book)
    Includes index.
    ISBN 0-516-01056-5
    1. Otters–Juvenile literature. [1. Otters.]
I. Title.
QL737.C25L465    1994
599.74'447–dc20
                                                        93-33515
                                                        CIP
                                                        AC

# TABLE OF CONTENTS

A river otter pauses on the ice of a winter pond.

# OTTERS AROUND THE WORLD

The ancestors of otters probably lived on land. Over millions of years, they adapted to life in the water. The two main kinds of otters are river otters

4

Sea otters like to float on their back.

and sea otters. They are
found on every continent
except Australia and
Antarctica.

The American river otter
is found throughout most
of North and South

America. Sea otters live along the Pacific coast of North America, the Aleutian Islands off Alaska, and northeastern Asia.

Otters are mammals. They are covered with fur and nurse their young with milk. They breathe oxygen from the air. Otters are related to skunks, mink, weasels, martens, and badgers.

Otter relatives include weasels (left) and skunks (right).

Martens (left), badgers (top right), and mink (bottom right) are also related to otters.

Otters belong to the weasel family—Mustelidae. The scientific name for the American river otter is *Lutra canadensis*. The sea otter is *Enhydra lutris*.

7

River otters dive to the bottom of ponds and streams to look for food.

# RIVER OTTERS

River otters live near rivers and lakes. They spend much of their time swimming. Otters feed on fish and small animals such as crayfish. They can

River otters are mainly fish eaters.

crush shells and slice fish
with their strong sharp teeth.
They also eat snakes, clams,
snails, frogs, and even
earthworms.

The river otter's tail is long and tapered.

River otters have a small, flattened head, long whiskers, and a thick neck. They have a powerful, tapered tail that makes up one-third of their length.

Adult male river otters weigh 10 to 30 pounds (4.5 to 14 kilograms). They measure up to 4.5 feet (1.4 meters) long, including the tail. Females are somewhat smaller.

Otters can hold their breath and stay under water up to four minutes.

River otters have good
eyesight and a very keen
sense of smell.

They make many
different sounds. They
chatter, chuckle, grunt,
snort, and growl. They
also warn other otters of
danger with a shrill
whistle.

Otters' feet have webbing between the toes so that the feet act like paddles in the water.

# LEGS, FEET, AND EARS

Otters have short legs with five toes on each foot. Elastic skin called webbing between the toes helps them swim. Except for pads on their toes and soles, their feet are covered with fur.

Otters use their front paws like hands to handle food and other objects.

They use their paws to feel for crayfish under rocks in muddy riverbeds. They hold food in their front paws while they eat it.

Special muscles allow otters to close their small ears and nostrils to keep water out.

Otters resting on a floating log

# OTTER FUR

The fur on the river otter's sides and back is a rich black-brown color. The fur on the belly is lighter, and the chin and throat are grayish. Coarse guard hairs cover their thick, soft underfur.

15

An otter grooming its fur. Otters shed their hairs a few at a time, not all at once like some animals, so their fur coat is always thick and full.

River otters take good care of their beautiful fur. They groom their coats every day. They roll on the ground to dry their fur and keep it waterproof. Their fur protects them from the cold.

# RIVER OTTER TERRITORIES

River otters mark their territory by rubbing musk on logs and stones. Musk is a sweet-smelling liquid produced by scent glands near their tail.

Otters have dens, or homes, on land, in the banks of rivers and ponds. Sometimes they take over

Florida river otters catch up on their rest before hunting for food.

an abandoned muskrat or beaver den dug into a riverbank.

Otters are nocturnal animals. They are active at night and usually sleep in the daytime. When they are not hunting for food or

grooming their beautiful fur,
otters love to run around.

They wrestle and chase
each other. Otters like to
slide down a slippery
slope into a pond or
stream. Then they race up
the slope so that they can
slide down again.

River otters like to chase each
other underwater (left). In winter,
they slide down snowy banks (below).

A male and female otter drinking water. They will stay together for part of the year, but the mother drives the male away when the pups are ready to be born.

# RIVER OTTER PUPS

Otters must be at least two years old to mate. The mating season usually comes at the end of winter. Two months later, up to four pups, or cubs, are born. The pups' eyes are closed for five weeks. They have no teeth. They feed on their mother's milk.

The mother otter takes care of the pups for almost

These river otter pups are about two months old.

a year. When she takes the
pups out of the den, the
father otter may join his
family. The parents teach
their pups to swim, dive,
catch food, groom their fur—
and slide down slopes.

# ENEMIES

For hundreds of years, river otters were killed for their thick, beautiful fur. It was used to make coats, hats, and other articles of clothing.

Today, many governments have laws against otter hunting. But humans are still one of the otter's worst enemies. Many of these wonderful animals are killed by cars when they cross roads at night.

# SEA OTTERS

Sea otters are truly amazing animals. They spend most of their time in the ocean floating on masses of seaweed.

Male sea otters measure at least 4.5 feet (1.4 meters), including their long, broad tail. They usually weigh from 70 to 80 pounds (32 to 36 kilograms). Females measure almost 4 feet (1.2

A sea otter floating on its back near the rocky shore

meters), and weigh about 45 pounds (20 kilograms).

The fur coat of a sea otter looks like it is several sizes too big. They have white hair around the face and head, and long white whiskers.

# LIVING IN THE SEA

Kelp is a brown seaweed with large stems that grow up to 200 feet (61 meters) long. Kelp beds grow along the Pacific coast like underwater forests.

Sea otters like to live together in kelp beds.

A raft of sea otters

They form groups of up to one hundred called rafts. Males form one raft. Females and pups form another raft.

A sleeping sea otter floats in its bed of kelp.

Sea otters eat, sleep,
and swim on their back.
When they sleep, they
float on strands of kelp
that hold them securely.
They are completely
relaxed. Their head is out
of the water and their
forepaws rest on their
chest. Their flipper-like

When the sea otter swims on its back, it uses its broad hind feet like flippers to paddle itself along.

hind feet and their tail stick up out of the water.

Sea otters comb their fur carefully with their claws. Then they blow into the fur to make it fluffy. The trapped air in their fur helps keep them afloat.

# USING TOOLS

Sea otters like to eat abalones, sea urchins, mussels, and other shellfish they find on the seafloor. If a shellfish is attached to a rock, the sea otter picks up a stone in its forepaws and hammers the shell until the shellfish comes loose. Then the otter tucks the shellfish in a fold of skin under one of its forelegs.

The otter "fishes" until it has several shellfish stored

Sea otter eating a sea urchin (left). Otters use a small stone like a tool to open the shells of sea animals (right).

under its leg. Then it puts the stone under its other leg and rises to the surface.

Floating on its back, the otter puts the stone on its chest and holds a shellfish in its forepaws. Then it pounds the shellfish against the stone to crack the shell. An adult otter eats 15 to 20 pounds (7 to 9 kilograms) of seafood each day.

When it has eaten its fill, the otter simply rolls over to dump the shells, the scraps, and the stone. Seagulls wait for the scraps.

Seagulls pick up the scraps from an otter's meal.

A young sea otter pup rides on its mother's chest.

# MATING AND BIRTH

Sea otters mate at any time of the year. The male and female stay together for about three days at mating time. A single pup is born—either in the water or on land.

33

Older pups stay near their mother. They are learning to take care of their fur, to swim and dive, and to find their own food.

Female sea otters take very good care of their young. The mother cradles the pup on her chest, holding it with her forelegs. She fluffs its fur.

# CARING FOR THE PUP

The pup depends on its mother for the first year. It drinks her rich milk.

When she dives down to hunt for food, the mother otter makes sure the pup is held securely in the kelp. Pups cry while their mother is gone.

Pups can float as soon as they are born. However, they must practice swimming and diving for a

Sea otter mother and pup eating crabs

long time before they can
live on their own.

When the pup is old
enough to eat solid food,
the mother hunts for food
for both of them. Soon the
pup tries diving down to
find its own food.

This painting shows a storm
wrecking Vitus Bering's ships.

# SEA OTTERS IN DANGER

Sea otters were unknown
to Europeans until 1741.
At that time, Vitus Bering,
a captain in the Russian
navy, sailed past the
Aleutian Islands. Bad storms
forced him to land on

an island, where Bering and some of his men died.

The survivors saw strange animals in kelp beds off the shore. They were sea otters and they were not afraid of the men. The sailors killed many for food, and used their fur to make clothing and fur blankets.

Hunters used traps to catch river otters on land.

The discovery of the sea otters led to exploration of vast areas of the northern Pacific Ocean. Otter fur became very popular in China, and Russian ships brought back thousands of otter pelts.

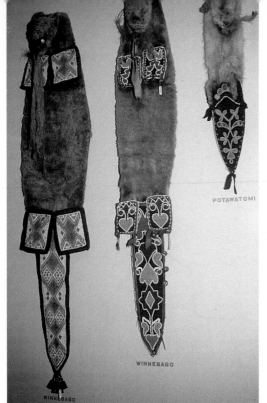

WINNEBAGO

POTAWATOMI

WINNEBAGO

Native Americans of the midwestern United States used otter skins to make decorated bags (left). The Kwakiutl people of the Pacific Northwest made this wooden bowl in the shape of a sea otter (below).

Sea otters were also abundant off the California coast. The Spanish settlers in the mild climate of California did not need warm fur. But they traded the otter pelts to Europeans for other things that they needed.

Soon the sea otters off the California coast were threatened with extinction.

In 1911 the United States, Russia, Japan, and Great Britain agreed not to hunt seals and sea otters. By that time, the sea otter was thought to be extinct. However, a few animals were hidden in bays and coves in the Aleutian Islands.

In 1931 a scientist saw a mother sea otter with her pup on her chest. They were in a kelp bed off the coast of Amchitka Island. There are now over 40,000 sea otters in the Aleutians. Some have been moved to the coasts of Oregon, Washington, and British Columbia to make sure they have enough food.

By 1937, sea otters had reappeared off the coast

Monterey Bay, California, is once again the home of sea otters. The bay has huge beds of kelp and many kinds of shellfish for the otters to eat.

of California between Big
Sur and Monterey. Today,
about 1,000 sea otters live
in California waters.

Species of otters around the world include the giant otter (above)
of South America and the small-clawed otter of Asia (below).

Sea otters are coming back to their old homes
in the waters of the northern Pacific Ocean.

There are nine species
of otters throughout the
world. Each species of
these playful animals has
found ways to survive in
its special environment—the
watery world of the otter. **45**

# WORDS YOU SHOULD KNOW

**abalone** (ab • uh • LONE • ee) – a shellfish with a large, flat shell

**abandoned** (uh • BAN • dund) – left behind; deserted

**adapt** (uh • DAPT) – to change to fit new living conditions

**Aleutian Islands** (uh • LOO • shin EYE • lindz) – a chain of islands in the northern Pacific Ocean off the coast of Alaska

**ancestors** (AN • sess • terz) – family members who lived earlier in history

**continent** (KAHN • tih • nent) – one of the earth's large landmasses

**crayfish** (KRAY • fish) – a hard-shelled water animal that looks like a small lobster

**elastic** (ih • LASS • tik) – easily stretched

*Enhydra lutris* (en • HY • druh LOO • tris) – the scientific name for the sea otter

**environment** (en • VY • run • mint) – the things that surround a plant or an animal; the lands and waters of the earth

**exploration** (ex • pluh • RAY • shun) – going to new places to find out what is there

**extinct** (ex • TINKT) – no longer living

**glands** (GLANDZ) – a special body part that makes substances the body can use or give off

**guard hairs** (GARD HAIRZ) – long hairs in the outer fur of animals

**kelp** (KELP) – a tough brown seaweed with very large, long leaves

*Lutra canadensis* (LOO • truh kan • uh • DEN • siss) – the scientific name for the North American river otter

**mammal** (MAM • il) – one of a group of warm-blooded animals that have hair and nurse their young with milk

**musk** (MUHSK)–a substance with a strong and lasting odor

**mussel** (MUH • sil)–a small water animal that has a hard, two-piece shell

**Mustelidae** (mus • TEL • ih • day)–the family of animals that includes otters, skunks, mink, weasels, martens, and badgers

**nocturnal** (nahk • TER • nil)–awake and active at night

**oxygen** (OX • ih • jin)–a gas found in the air that humans and animals need to breathe

**pelt** (PEHLT)–the skin of an animal with the fur attached

**scientific name** (sy • en • TIF • ik  NAYM)–a name, usually from the Latin language, that scientists give to a plant or an animal

**sea urchin** (SEE  UR • chin)–a small water animal that is covered with sharp spines

**seagull** (SEE • guhl)–a bird with long narrow wings that lives on or near the water

**seaweed** (SEE • weed)–a plant that grows in water

**settlers** (SET • lerz)–people who come to a new country and establish farms or other homes there

**shellfish** (SHELL • fish)–an animal that lives in water and that is covered by a shell

**species** (SPEE • sheez)–a group of related plants or animals that are able to interbreed

**survivor** (ser • VY • ver)–a person left alive after a disaster, such as a fire or shipwreck

**tapered** (TAY • perd)–wide at one end and gradually narrowing toward the other end

**territory** (TAIR • ih • tor • ee)–an area with definite boundaries that an animal lives in

**whiskers** (WISS • kerz)–long, stiff hairs on the upper lip

# INDEX

## About the Author

Emilie U. Lepthien received her BA and MS degrees and certificate in school administration from Northwestern University. She taught upper-grade science and social studies, wrote and narrated science programs for the Chicago Public Schools' station WBEZ, and was principal in Chicago, Illinois, for twenty years. She received the American Educator's Medal from Freedoms Foundation.

She is a member of Delta Kappa Gamma Society International, Chicago Principals' Association, Illinois Women's Press Association, National Federation of Press Women, and AAUW.

She has written books in the Enchantment of the World, New True Books, and America the Beautiful series.